# CHICKENHARE™

## The House of Klaus

# CHICKENHARE™

## The House of Klaus

STORY AND ARTWORK BY

CHRIS GRINE

*Designed by* CHRIS GRINE

*Edited by* SHAWNA GORE

*Assistant Editor* JEMIAH JEFFERSON

*Publisher* MIKE RICHARDSON

Published by Dark Horse Books
A division of Dark Horse Comics, Inc.
10956 SE Main St.
Milwaukie, OR 97222

September 2006
First edition
ISBN-10: 1-59307-574-X
ISBN-13: 978-1-59307-574-3

1 3 5 7 9 10 8 6 4 2



Printed in Canada

COME ON, BARLEY. YOU DON'T REALLY WANT TO SELL US TO THIS WEIRD COLLECTOR GUY, RIGHT?
OH YES I DO!
AND SHUT YER DANG MOUTHS. I TOLD YA ALREADY WE DON'T WANT TO BE NOTICED OUT HERE!

BY WHAT, SNOWMEN?
HA
HA
HA
HA

*SHROMPH*, YOU ***IDIOTS***, NOT SNOWMEN! NASTY CRITTERS WITH RAZOR SHARP TEETH.

SHRIMP? OUT ***HERE?***

OH YES, LAUGH IT UP WHILE YA STILL CAN.

MR. KLAUS AIN'T YER AVERAGE COLLECTOR OF EXOTIC ANIMALS, NO SIR. HE FANCIES HIMSELF TO BE A TAXIDERMIST, AND BETWEEN YOU AND ME, HE AIN'T A VERY GOOD ONE.

HELLO, CHICKENHARE.

WHAT IN THE...

I NEED YOU TO HELP ME.

HEY ABE, CHECK OUT THIS FUNNY-LOOKING GOAT OVER HERE.

WHERE?
RIGHT OVER THERE.

THAT'S WEIRD. I COULD HAVE SWORN I SAW A GOAT WEARING A TOP HAT.

THIS GUY'S GONNA GUT YA BOTH, AND THEN STUFF YA FULL'A FLUFF!

AFTER THAT, HE'LL DRESS YA UP REAL PRETTY.

HMM...
OH, I'M SORRY! WERE YOU STILL TALKING?

GRRRRRRR!
I HOPE HE TORTURES *BOTH* OF YOU BEFORE HE KILLS YA.

NOW DO YOU *REALLY* WANT THAT ON YOUR CONSCIENCE?
I SURE WOULDN'T.

MAYBE HE'LL EVEN LET ME HELP.

YOU *SUCK*, MR. BARLEY!

WHY DON'T MY PETS RETURN MY LOVE, MR. FINGERBONES?
PERHAPS SIR, IT'S BECAUSE THEY'VE ALL BEEN STUFFED?
WELL THEY DON'T LEAVE ME MUCH CHOICE DO THEY? IT'S THE ONLY WAY I CAN BE SURE THEY WON'T LEAVE ME...
...LIKE HE DID.

THERE.

WHY DID HE LEAVE ME, *FINGERBONES?*

MIGHT IT HAVE BEEN THE *INCESSANT BEATINGS* HE RECEIVED, SIR?

POOR LITTLE *MR. BUTTONS*, HOW I LOVED TO DRESS HIM UP ALL FANCY.
DO YOU THINK HE'S STILL OUT THERE SOMEWHERE, *FINGERBONES*?
NOT LIKELY, SIR. IT'S BEEN NEARLY FORTY YEARS.
HAS IT BEEN THAT LONG?
IT SEEMS LIKE ONLY YESTERDAY I WAS BEATING HIM FOR EATING THE BUTTONS OFF MY BEST JACKET.
BUTTONS

BUTTONS WERE HIS *FAVORITE*.

I WON'T LET IT HAPPEN AGAIN!

I'LL NEVER LET ANOTHER ONE LEAVE ME!
NEVER!
BUT TONS

YOUR LOVE FOR ANIMALS IS TRULY STAGGERING, SIR.

SCARY, ISN'T IT?
INDEED.

DO YOU THINK THIS *KLAUS* GUY IS ***REALLY*** GONNA STUFF US, CHICKENHARE?
MAYBE HE WON'T EVEN WANT US, *ABE*.
NOT LIKELY.

THIS FELLA'S INTO THE RARE AND EXOTIC STUFF.

AND YOU TWO'RE 'BOUT AS RARE AND EXOTIC AS THEY COME.

LOOK, I DON'T WANT ANOTHER *INCIDENT* LIKE *LAST* TIME I WAS HERE, SO YOU TWO KEEP YER MOUTHS *SHUT*.
WHY, WHAT HAPPENED LAST TIME?
WELL, LET'S JUST SAY I MADE A JOKE ABOUT HIS GOAT PORTRAIT AND HE NEARLY *KILLED* ME!

IS THAT RIGHT?

THUNK
THUNK
THUNK

ARE YOU EXPECTING GUESTS, SIR?

IT'S *BARLEY*, AND HE'S LATE.
SHOW HIM IN HERE, *FINGERBONES*.

VERY GOOD, SIR.

KLAK

BE A GOOD BUTLER, *FINGERBONES*, AND TELL *KLAUS* I'M HERE.
HE *ALREADY* KNOWS, AND HE INFORMS ME YOU ARE ***QUITE*** LATE.

IS HE MAD?

AS A ***HATTER***.

YOU'RE *LATE*, *BARLEY!*
S-SORRY, *MR. KLAUS.*

LET'S TALK IN THE DRAWING ROOM.
THANK YOU, *MR. KLAUS.*

NOT A PEEP!
UNDERSTAND?
COMPLETELY.
YEP.

HEY *BARLEY*, IS *THAT* THE PORTRAIT?
BU
YEP, THAT'S THE ONE, AND I...

...THOUGHT I TOLD *YOU* TO KEEP QUIET?

IS THIS *IT*, *BARLEY*?
THIS LOOKS LIKE A RABBIT AND A STUPID TURTLE TO ME, NOTHING RARE OR EXOTIC ABOUT EITHER OF THEM!

ON THE *CONTRARY*, KLAUS.
THESE ARE LIKE *NO* ANIMAL YOU'VE *EVER* SEEN BEFORE!

I'M LISTENING.

TAKE THIS ONE FOR EXAMPLE.

THIS IS *NO* ORDINARY TURTLE. THIS IS A *RARE WHISKERED CHELONAI*, MORE COMMONLY KNOWN AS THE *BEARDED BOX-TURTLE*. AND THE ONLY ONE KNOWN TO EXIST!

THAT'S THE *LAMEST* EXCUSE FOR AN EXOTIC ANIMAL I'VE *EVER* SEEN!

MOVING RIGHT ALONG--I THINK YOU'RE *REALLY* GONNA *LOVE* THIS NEXT ONE.
FLING
GET AWAY FROM ME, PIG!

I LIKE THIS ONE *BETTER* ALREADY!

SNAP

THOUGH IT MAY *APPEAR* TO BE AN ORDINARY *RABBIT,* TAKE A *CLOSER* LOOK.
IT HAS THE EARS AND BODY OF A RABBIT, BUT IT *ALSO* HAS FEATHERS AND THE LEGS OF A *CHICKEN!*

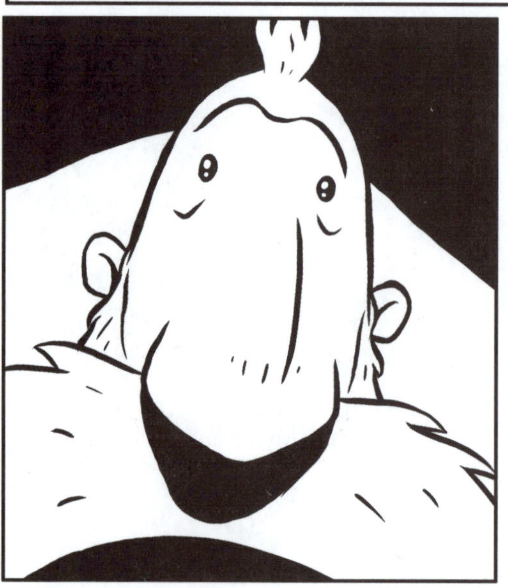

WHOO-HOO! HOW MUCH FOR THAT ONE?

ABE, ARE YOU HURT?
JUST MY FEELINGS. WHY?
I'M AFRAID THEY ONLY COME AS A PAIR, AND THEY WON'T BE CHEAP.

I HAVE AN IDEA. BE READY TO RUN WHEN I TELL YOU TO, OK?

GOOD, BECAUSE I'M READY TO LEAVE.

EXCUSE ME, *MR. KLAUS?*
WHAT ARE YOU DOING?

***YES,*** MY LITTLE CHICKEN-BUNNY?

I JUST WANTED TO TELL YOU THAT *I* DON'T THINK YOUR GOAT PORTRAIT IS ***NEARLY*** AS GUT-WRENCHINGLY ***HIDEOUS*** AS MR. BARLEY WAS TELLING US IT WAS.

YOU'RE WELCOME.

HIDEOUS IS IT, BARLEY?

M-MR. KLAUS, HE'S LYING! I NEVER S-SAID THAT!

ABE, RUN!

I THOUGHT I MADE MYSELF VERY CLEAR LAST TIME, BARLEY!
ACK! YOU DID! ACK!

I CAN'T *BELIEVE* YOU JUST DID THAT!

I CAN'T BELIEVE IT *WORKED*!

WUMP

AND JUST *WHERE* DO YOU TWO THINK YOU'RE GOING?

CHICKENHARE?
ARE YOU OKAY?

LEAVE HIM ALONE.
STOP.
TAKE THEM UPSTAIRS, PLUMMS.

I THINK YOUR BUDDY'S WAKING UP.
HEY, *CHICKENHARE*.

***CHICKENHARE***, ARE YOU ALL RIGHT?

***ABE***? WHAT ***HAPPENED***? WHERE ***ARE*** WE?

THEY PUT US IN CAGES--
--AND I THINK THAT ***JUST*** ABOUT COVERS IT.

WE NEED TO GET *OUTTA* HERE!
WELL BY ***ALL*** MEANS DON'T LET A LITTLE THING LIKE THAT ***METAL CAGE*** STOP YA.

WHO'S THIS GUY?
THAT'S BANJO. HE'S KINDUVA JERK.
WOW, THAT HURTS, ABE.
AND THAT'S MEG OVER THERE.
I GET THE FEELING SHE DOESN'T CARE MUCH FOR HIM EITHER.

HOW LONG HAVE THE TWO OF YOU BEEN *HERE?*

I'VE ACTUALLY LOST TRACK.

HAVE YOU TRIED TO ESCAPE?

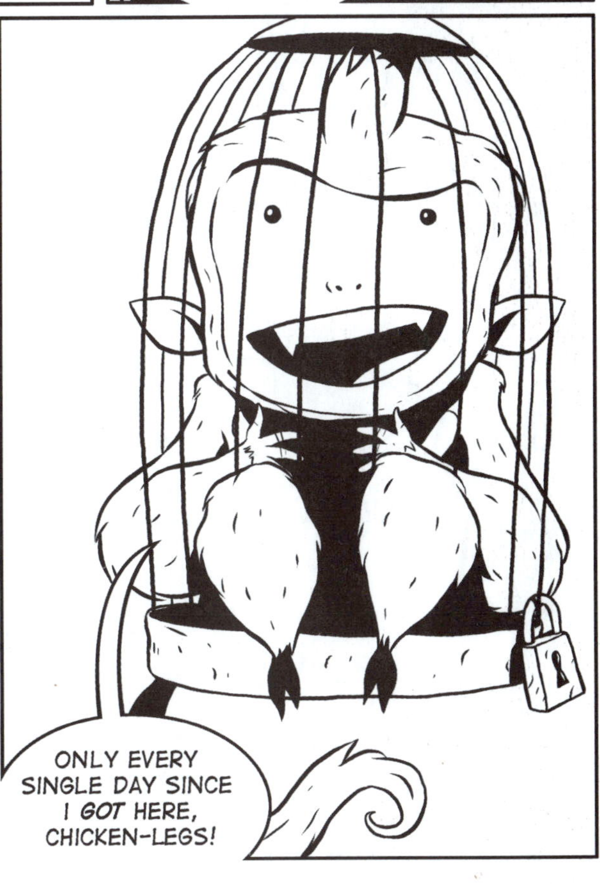
ONLY EVERY SINGLE DAY SINCE I *GOT* HERE, CHICKEN-LEGS!

SHHH!
HE'S COMING!

WHO'S COMING?
MR. PLUMMS, AND ALL OF HIS TIGHT LEOTARD-WEARING GLORY.
HE'S THE GUY YOU RAN INTO DOWNSTAIRS, CHICKENHARE.

BA-DOOM!

WELL, WELL, WELL. LOOK WHO'S *FINALLY* AWAKE.

I *DEMAND* THAT YOU *RELEASE* US!
UM... CHICKENHARE, *MAYBE* YOU SHOULD PLAY NICE.
BETTER *LISTEN* TO YOUR FRIEND, *CHICKENHARE*. IT WOULD BE A *SHAME* IF I HAD TO *HURT* SOMEBODY.

I DOUBT MR. KLAUS WOULD WANT YOU HURTING HIS FAVORITE NEW PET, TUBBY.

SLAP
NOW LET ME OUT!

YOU'RE RIGHT, I CAN'T HURT YOU...

...BUT I CAN HURT YOUR GREEN BUDDY OVER THERE.

WAIT!
PLUMMS, HOLD ON!
I'M SORRY!
TOO LATE!

CLANG!

LEAVE HIM ALONE!
YOU'RE PRETTY *TOUGH* AGAINST UNARMED TURTLES!

YOU WANT SOME *TOO*, MONKEY?

I'LL BE BACK FOR THE TURTLE *REAL* SOON. HE'S GOT A *DATE* WITH THE TAXIDERMIST.

*SUCKS* TO BE YOU, *GREENY*!

AND YOU'RE NEXT, *MONKEY*!
BOOM

WE GOTTA GET *OUTTA* HERE!

*ABE*. I'M *SO* SORRY. ARE YOU *OKAY*?
*ABE'S* IN HIS *HAPPY* PLACE.

HMM.
THAT'S *IT!*

I KNOW HOW TO FREE US!

ARE YOU KIDDING ME?

THE ROPE! IF WE CAN UNTIE IT, WE CAN ESCAPE!
UH...GUYS?

YEA, I FIGURED THAT OUT ABOUT TWO SECONDS AFTER I GOT HERE! WE CAN'T REACH IT.
YOU GUYS AREN'T GONNA BELIEVE THIS!
ABE! LET THE ADULTS TALK, OKAY?

WELL, MAYBE WE COULD *THROW* SOMETHING AT IT.
LIKE *WHAT?*
SERIOUSLY GUYS, *LOOK!*

JEEPERS-CRAPPERS, *ABE*! WE'RE TRYING TO...

AAAHHHHH!

I *KNOW!*
IT HAPPENED WHEN HE *HIT* MY CAGE!

GET DOWN THERE AND *UNTIE* THAT ROPE!
NO, WAIT!

IF HE UNTIES THAT ROPE ALL THE CAGES ARE GONNA COME CRASHING DOWN!

WOW, YOU'RE A FREAKIN' GENIUS, MEG! DID YOU COME UP WITH THAT ALL BY YOURSELF?

I WASN'T FINISHED, DEVIL!

LISTEN, AS SOON AS THESE CAGES HIT THE FLOOR PLUMMS IS GONNA COME RUNNING!

WE'LL DEAL WITH THAT IF IT HAPPENS, OKAY? LET'S JUST GET DOWN FIRST.
NO, I THINK MEG'S RIGHT.

OK, SO AFTER WE'RE DOWN, ABE, YOU GRAB THE KEYS AND OPEN OUR CAGES.
GOTCHA.
WHAT CAN I DO?

MEG, I'LL NEED YOU TO HELP ME WITH THAT WINDOW.

WHOA! WHAT'S ALL THIS TALK ABOUT LETTING HER OUT?

WHY WOULDN'T WE LET MEG OUT?

BECAUSE IF YOU LET HER OUT, SHE'S GONNA TRY TO KILL ME. THAT'S WHY.

COME ON! SHE'S *NOT* GONNA KILL YOU! *RIGHT*, *MEG?*

ACTUALLY...

OKAY, FINE! HOW ABOUT *THIS--ABE* AND I LEAVE YOU BOTH *HERE!*

OKAY, I WON'T KILL HIM... FOR NOW.
BETTER *GET* THAT IN *WRITING*.

THAT'S *RIGHT*, MR. SMILES-A-LOT. DADDY HAS THREE NEW BROTHERS AND SISTERS FOR YOU TO *PLAY* WITH.
IT *WOULD* HAVE BEEN *FOUR*, BUT I'VE DECIDED TO MAKE THE *TURTLE* INTO AN ASH TRAY.

EXCUSE ME, *MR. KLAUS*.
WHO'S DADDY'S FAVORITE WIDDLE BEAR?

WHAT IS IT, *PLUMMS?*
I THOUGHT YOU'D LIKE TO KNOW THE RABBIT THING IS *AWAKE*.

THANK YOU. GO PREPARE THE OPERATING ROOM.
I'VE DECIDED TO DO IT FIRST AFTER ALL.

WITH *PLEASURE*, SIR.

CLANG! CLUNG! BOOM!
WHAT IN THE...?

BETTER NOT BE MAKING A *MESS* UP THERE!

CRASSH!

BA-DOOM!
WHAT'S GOING ON IN HERE?

NO!

NO!

NO!
NO!
NO!
NO!
NO!

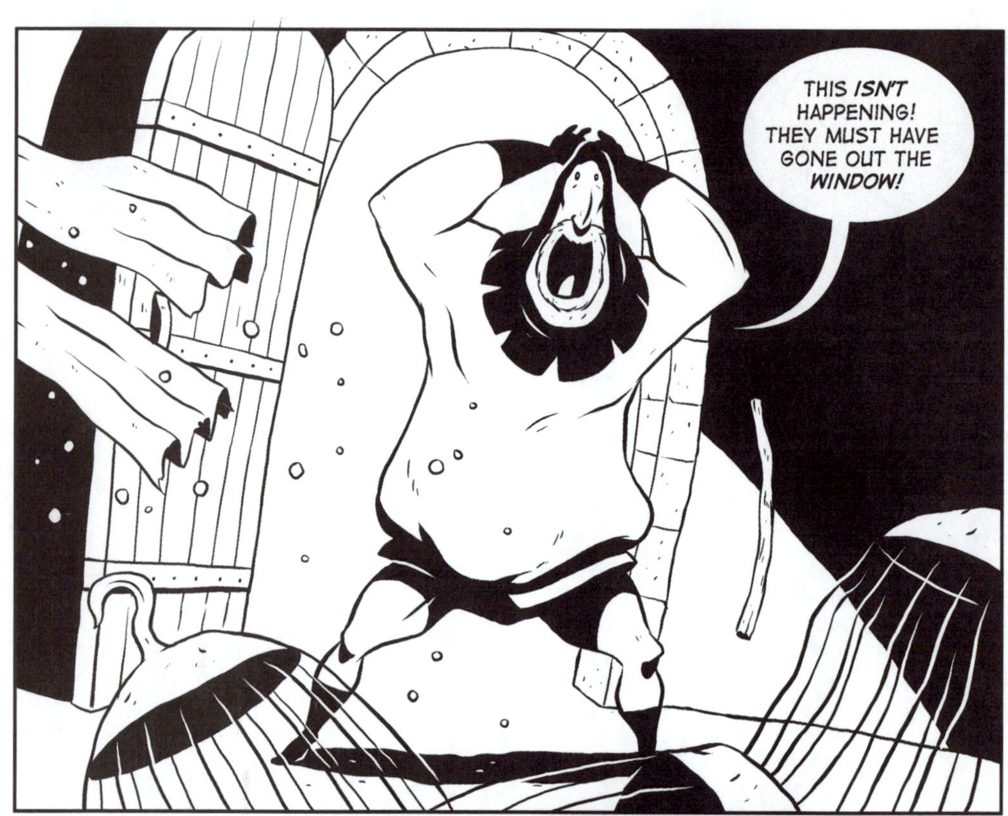
THIS *ISN'T* HAPPENING! THEY MUST HAVE GONE OUT THE *WINDOW!*

HEY, *WAIT* A *SECOND!* THERE'S NO WAY THEY COULD ESCAPE OUT THAT WINDOW.

IT'S A FORTY FOOT DROP.

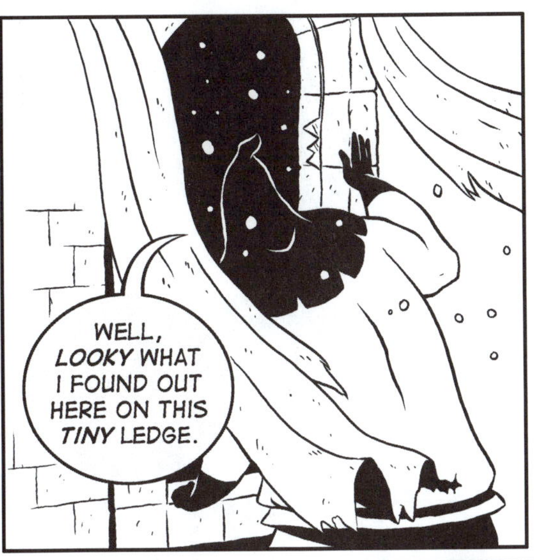
WELL, *LOOKY* WHAT I FOUND OUT HERE ON THIS *TINY* LEDGE.

SO MUCH FOR THAT BIG *ESCAPE* PLAN, HUH?

WHY DON'T YOU JUST COME BACK INSIDE. THERE'S NOWHERE ELSE TO GO, EXCEPT DOWN. AND I *DOUBT* YOU WANT TO GO *THAT* WAY.

WUMP!

aaHHH!

WHEN I TOLD YOU TO KNOCK HIM *OUT*, I DIDN'T MEAN *OUT* THE *WINDOW!*
I IMPROVISED.

DADDY HAS TO GO TO WORK NOW, SO...

aaHHHH!

NOW WHAT?
WELL, I GUESS WE SHOULD FIND ANOTHER WAY OUT.

I THINK THE MAIN ENTRANCE IS JUST DOWNSTAIRS.

SOMEBODY'S COMING!
QUICK, BEHIND THE DOOR!

WHAT'S GOING ON IN HERE?!

NO!

NOOOOOO!
cRReeeaak

HEY!

WAY TO GO, *ABE!*

HEY, GET BACK HERE! STOP!

OH NO, IT'S *FINGERBONES!*

YOU *VERMIN* AREN'T GOING *ANYWHERE!*

MEG! BANJO! THAT'S ENOUGH, WE NEED TO GO!
THIS IS YOUR LUCKY DAY, BUTLER!

COME ON!

I WON'T LET YOU LEAVE ME!

SIR! WAIT!

whoa!

OW! MY *LUNGS!*

YOU *WON'T* ESCAPE ME *THAT* EASILY!
KEEP RUNNING!

IS IT A TAD COLDER THAN YOU'RE USED TO, DEVIL?
HMM-HMM-HM-HMM
I'M FINE, THANKS.

HOW ARE YOU STAYIN' SO CHIPPER, ABE?
IT'S FREEZING OUT HERE!
MY HAT AND THESE SWEET GLOVES ARE KEEPING ME TOASTY!
YOU DON'T SAY?

YOU ARE SO RIGHT ABOUT THESE GLOVES, ABE. THEY ARE TOASTY!
SHUT UP!

YOU ARE A JERK!
HEY, I LET HIM KEEP THE HAT.

ONLY BECAUSE IT DIDN'T FIT!

THANKS ANYWAY, MEG. IT'S NOT WORTH KILLING HIM OVER MY GLOVES.
I'LL LEAVE IT ON THE TABLE, JUST IN CASE YOU CHANGE YOUR MIND.

CHICKENHARE.

HELP ME, CHICKENHARE.
WHAT IN THE...?

YOU JUST *TRY* IT, *MEG*!

EVERYONE STAY CLOSE. IT'S GETTING *WORSE* OUT HERE AND WE *DON'T* WANT TO BE SEPARATED.
EXCEPT *BANJO*!
WHAT SIZE WAS THAT HAT AGAIN?

HEY BANJO, ANY CHANCE I COULD GET THOSE GLOVES BACK?
UM.. NOPE, PROBABLY NOT.
WHY NOT?
I GOT RID OF THEM ABOUT FIVE HOURS BACK.
WHAT?!
WELL, WHAT WAS I SUPPOSED TO DO, ABE?
MY HANDS WERE GETTING REALLY SWEATY AND PRUNEY.

HEY, THAT'S THE CAVE CHICKENHARE AND I PASSED ON THE WAY IN.
I THINK BARLEY SAID IT WASN'T SAFE, THOUGH. SOMETHING ABOUT SHROMPH.
WHO CARES! I'M FREEZING!
WHAT DO YOU THINK WE SHOULD DO, CHICKENHARE?
HEY, WHERE IS HE?

CHICKENHARE!
CHICKENHARE!
I'M REALLY COLD AND I WANNA GO INTO THE CAVE!

C'MON, *ABE*. I'M SURE HE'LL SHOW UP.

WHAT DID YOU SAY LIVED IN HERE, *ABE*? ***SHRIMP?***

*SHROMPH, YOU IDIOT.*

YOU AGAIN!

OKAY, I'M HERE. WHAT DO YOU WANT?

I NEED YOU TO FIND ME.

I JUST DID! I'M STANDING. RIGHT IN FRONT OF YOU!
COME CLOSER.

WELL, AT *LEAST* I WASN'T IMAGINING THINGS EARLIER BACK ON THE...
...ROAD!

CRUNCH
CRACK

I HOPE THAT WASN'T A *BONE*.

IF IT *WAS*, IT WAS MOST LIKELY *MINE*.
WHAT?

PLEASE, SIR. *DON'T* MAKE ME GO WITH YOU. I'M IN *UNBEARABLE* PAIN.

FASTER!
CRACK

MR. KLAUS, PLEASE!
FASTER, BEEF!
FASTER, PATTI!

SIR, I'M SURE I MUST BE BLEEDING INTERNALLY!

YOU SHOULD HAVE THOUGHT ABOUT THAT BEFORE YOU LET THEM ESCAPE!

IT'S BEEN HOURS.

I DON'T THINK HE'S COMING, *ABE*!

YOU GUYS DON'T *THINK* THAT TAXIDERMIST GUY GOT HIM, *DO* YOU?
I *HOPE* NOT.

*JUST* IN *CASE* THOUGH, MAYBE WE SHOULD MOVE *DEEPER* INTO THE CAVE.

I THINK WE'RE LOST.
AT LEAST IT'S GETTING WARMER, RIGHT?
ALWAYS LOOKING ON THE BRIGHT SIDE.
I TRY.
WOULD YOU TWO LIKE TO BE ALONE...
...TO KISS?

YOU'LL *NOT* SPEAK TO ME IN SUCH A WAY, **DEVIL!**

I'LL **SPEAK** HOW I **WANT!**

CUT IT OUT! WE DON'T WANT TO ATTRACT ANY ATTENTION!
SHE STARTED IT!
CRUNCH
SNAP
STOP IT! GUYS, STOP!
WHY SHOULD WE?
SEE FOR YOURSELVES.

WELL, *THESE* GUYS DON T LOOK *ANYTHING* LIKE *SHRIMP!*

YOU COULD HAVE WARNED ME, YOU KNOW.

WOW! THAT WAS SOME FALL.

WELL I'M JUST SO HAPPY I COULD ENTERTAIN YOU, GOAT!
I COULD HAVE DIED!

I'M HAPPY YOU DIDN'T DIE.
THAT WOULD HAVE *REALLY* MESSED UP MY PLANS.
I SURE WOULD *HATE* TO MESS UP YOUR GOAT PLANS.

WHAT BROKE MY FALL?
THAT WOULD BE MY BODY.

YOUR WHAT?

HOW CAN THIS BE YOUR BODY WHEN YOU'RE...
...YOU'RE DEAD.
THAT WOULD EXPLAIN QUITE A BIT.
FORTY YEARS AGO I ESCAPED FROM MY CRUEL MASTER, ONLY TO FALL INTO THIS HOLE AND BREAK MY LEGS. UNABLE TO MOVE, I EVENTUALLY STARVED TO DEATH DOWN HERE.
YOU'RE TALKING ABOUT KLAUS! YOU'RE MR. BUTTONS!
THAT'S RIGHT.
BUT WAIT, YOU HAVE AN UDDER. SO THAT MAKES YOU A MRS. NOT A MR.
KLAUS WAS TOO STUPID TO REALIZE THAT.

SO IF *YOU'RE* DEAD, WHAT ARE YOU DOING HANGING AROUND *HERE?*

UNFINISHED BUSINESS...
...AND THAT ISN'T A *CHAIR*.

OH! RIGHT! SORRY.

NO PROBLEM. COME WITH ME. I'LL EXPLAIN EVERYTHING. AND BRING MY BODY.

THIS JUST KEEPS GETTING BETTER AND BETTER.

WHY EXACTLY AM I DRAGGING THIS HAIRY POPSICLE YOU CALL A BODY AGAIN?
WE NEED TO THAW IT OUT.
WHAT THE HECK FOR?
SO IT MOVES BETTER.
WHY DOES IT NEED TO MOVE BETTER?...
...OH MAN, YOU'RE PLANNING ON GETTING BACK IN HERE, AREN'T YOU?
THAT'S THE IDEA, YES.

WAIT, DO YOU HEAR VOICES?

OH CRAP!

BUTTONS! GET DOWN, QUICK!

WE CAN TAKE'EM!
ARE YOU INSANE?
HE MUST BE TRACKING ABE AND THE OTHERS. I NEED TO WARN THEM.
THEY'RE IN SERIOUS DANGER.

THEY CAME THIS WAY, AND NOT TOO LONG AGO BY THE LOOKS OF THESE TRACKS.
UNHITCH YOURSELVES, BOYS. WE'LL BE TRAVELING ON *FOOT* FROM HERE ON OUT.
YES SIR, *MR. KLAUS*.

THE TRACKS LEAD UP THERE, TOWARDS THAT CAVE.
LET'S GET MOVING.

BUT SIR, THOSE CAVES ARE CRAWLING WITH SHROMPH!

THAT'S THE WAY WE'RE GOING, FINGERBONES!
ALL OF US!

BUT SIR, I'M REALLY IN NO CONDITION FOR SPELUNKING!

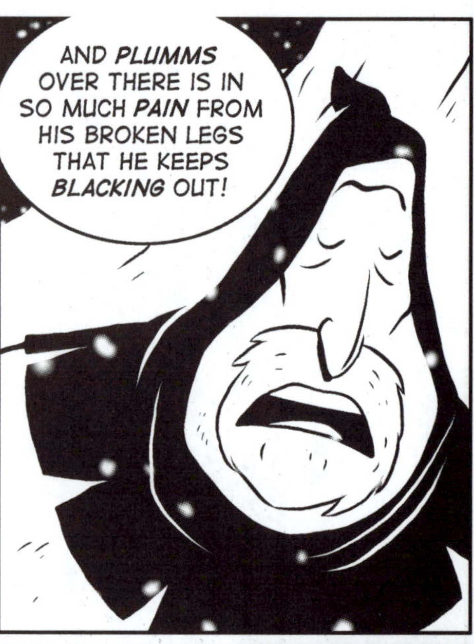
AND PLUMMS OVER THERE IS IN SO MUCH PAIN FROM HIS BROKEN LEGS THAT HE KEEPS BLACKING OUT!

I DON'T WANT ANY EXCUSES, FINGERBONES. UNLESS YOU WANT ME TO PERSONALLY BREAK EVERY BONE IN YOUR BODY,YOU BETTER GET BOTH YOU AND PLUMMS MOVING!

THIS SHOULD BE GOOD.
NO DOUBT.

HURRY IT UP, FINGERBONES.
AAAGGH! MY LEGS!

IT'S LIKE CARRYING A GIGANTIC SACK OF STINKY OLD POTATOES.

IS THERE ANOTHER WAY INTO THOSE CAVES?
WHAT ABOUT MY *BODY?*

IT'S GONNA HAVE TO THAW ON THE WAY, ALL RIGHT?

WE SHOULD HURRY.
AGREED.

IF YOUR FRIENDS *ARE* IN THOSE CAVES, IT'S A *GOOD* BET THE SHROMPH *FOUND* THEM ALREADY.
IS THAT *GOOD* OR *BAD?*

THAT DEPENDS.
ON WHAT?

IT DEPENDS ON *WHICH* ONE OF YOUR FRIENDS IS DOING THE TALKING.
CAN WE GO FASTER?

YOU JUST *COULDN'T* SHUT YOUR MOUTH, *COULD* YA?
HOW WAS *I* SUPPOSED TO KNOW *HE* WAS THEIR *LEADER?*
IT WAS THE *CROWN* THAT ACTUALLY GAVE IT AWAY FOR ME.

NOW, *WHICH* ONE OF YOU WOULD LIKE THE *HONOR* OF BEING THE FIRST COURSE?

PLEASE, YOUR MAJESTY, WE DIDN'T KNOW THESE CAVES BELONGED TO YOU AND...

SILENCE, FOOD!

WOW, *ABE*! THAT WAS *WAY* BETTER THAN I DID. *THANKS!*

YOU *MUST* LISTEN TO ME, YOUR MAJESTY!

A *LIKELY* STORY FROM ONE WHO WILLINGLY TRAVELS WITH A *KRAMPUS*.

YOU AND *ALL* OF YOUR PEOPLE ARE IN *TERRIBLE* DANGER!

HEY, BANJO. WHAT'S A KRAMPUS?
I THINK IT MEANS "BOSSY FEMALE."
WHAT?!
HE'S LYING, ABE! IT MEANS...
FWAP
I DIDN'T CATCH ALL OF THAT, MEG.
YOU KEEP THAT FILTHY TAIL OUT OF MY FACE, OR I'LL CUT IT OFF!
I THINK SOMEONE NEEDS A NAP.

THUNK

CRACK

YOU TWO BE *QUIET!*

I HAVE *DECIDED* TO LET THE *APPETIZER* EXPLAIN.

THANK YOU, YOUR MAJESTY.

I WILL ALLOW YOU *TEN* WORDS.

ONLY *TEN*?

ONLY EIGHT REMAIN.

YOU CAN'T COUNT *THOSE!*

DOWN TO *FOUR*.

UM...
THREE LEFT.

"UM" COUNTS?
KEEP UP THE GOOD WORK.
YOU HAVE BUT ONE WORD LEFT IN WHICH TO SAVE YOU AND YOUR DELICIOUS-LOOKING FRIENDS.
CHOOSE WISELY.
THINK ABE, THINK!
TAXIDERMIST!

WHAT? WHAT *ABOUT* HIM?

NO!
NOT AGAIN!

IT'S *TRUE*, YOUR MAJESTY. *KLAUS*, THE TAXIDERMIST, IS HUNTING FOR US AND HE'S PROBABLY ON HIS WAY HERE RIGHT *NOW!*

CAPTAIN! SEND *SCOUTS* TO *ALL* ENTRANCES. IF THEY'RE TELLING THE TRUTH WE HAVEN'T MUCH TIME!
YES, MAJESTY!

SO, WHY HAVEN'T YOU RETURNED TO YOUR BODY BEFORE *NOW?*

WHO SAID I HAVEN'T? THE TROUBLE IS ALL MY LEGS ARE BROKEN, NOT TO MENTION THE FACT THAT MY BODY WAS FROZEN SOLID. KINDA MAKES IT HARD TO DO MUCH, YA KNOW?

I GUESS THAT MAKES SENSE.

AND SO YOU'VE HUNG AROUND ALL THESE YEARS JUST TO GET REVENGE ON *KLAUS* FOR MISTREATING YOU?
THAT'S KINDA *SAD.*

PUT ME DOWN FOR A MINUTE.

Whoooops!
OOF!

*CHICKENHARE*, WHAT WE'RE DOING *ISN'T* ABOUT REVENGE AT ALL. IT'S ABOUT SAVING *INNOCENT* LIVES!

IT'S ABOUT STOPPING A *MAD-MAN!*

*KLAUS* HAS BEEN KILLING POOR SOULS FOR HOME DECOR PURPOSES HIS *ENTIRE* LIFE. WE HAVE TO STOP HIM!

IN CASE YOU HAVEN'T NOTICED WE'RE A BIT *OUTNUMBERED*, NOT TO MENTION THE FACT THAT I'VE NEVER BEEN IN A FIGHT AND YOU'RE DEAD!

HOW CAN WE POSSIBLY STOP HIM, GOAT?

YOU ASKED ME EARLIER WHY I'VE HUNG AROUND ALL THESE YEARS?

I DON'T THINK MY SPIRIT CAN REST UNTIL I STOP HIM.

IT'S MY FAULT HE HAS BECOME THE MONSTER HE IS TODAY. IF I HADN'T LEFT HIM, NONE OF THIS WOULD HAVE HAPPENED.
THIS IS CRAZY.

I JUST DON'T SEE *HOW* WE CAN DO THIS *ALONE*.
AND WE STILL NEED TO FIND MY FRIENDS.
WAIT! MY FRIENDS!

WHAT ABOUT THEM?

IF *THEY'LL* HELP US, MAYBE WE ACTUALLY *CAN* STOP *KLAUS*!

HOW MUCH FURTHER UNTIL WE REACH THE SHROMPH?

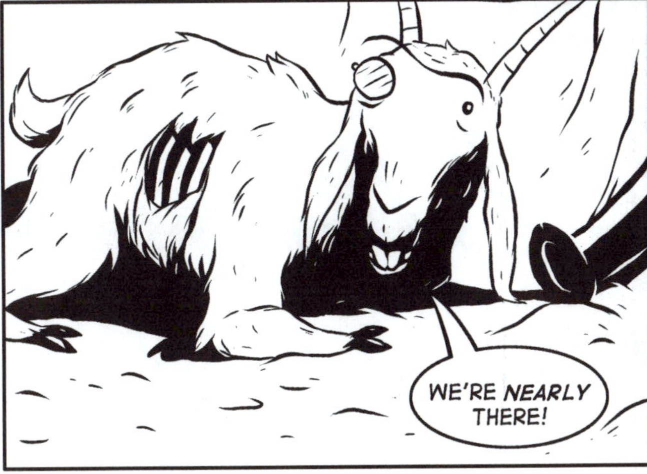
WE'RE *NEARLY* THERE!

THIS MUST BE WHERE THEY WENT IN. THERE'RE TRACKS ALL OVER THE PLACE.

LET'S PICK UP THE PACE, *FINGERBONES*!

UGGH.. *PLUMMS*, YOU FAT SACK OF *CRAP*!

I CAN'T CARRY THIS SLAB OF MEAT ANY FURTHER!

WHHaaG aaaGG! THe Pain!

THEN LEAVE HIM TO GUARD THE ENTRANCE!
DO YOU HEAR ME, *PLUMMS?*
NO ONE GETS OUT!
OH THANK YOU, SIR!

KICK

BY ALL MEANS, *MR. FINGERBONES*, LEAD THE WAY.

W-WHAT?
B-BUT *SIR*, THE *SHROMPH!* WHAT ABOUT THEM?

IF I WERE *YOU*, I'D BE MORE WORRIED ABOUT WHAT *I'M* GONNA DO TO YOU RIGHT NOW!
HEH-HEH!

AND IF I REFUSE?

I'LL MOUNT YOUR HEAD ABOVE THE FIREPLACE!

I BELIEVE YOU SAID I WAS FIRST?

KEEP QUIET!
THEY'RE HERE!

ARE WE ALMOST *THERE?*
SILENCE, KRAMPUS!

YOUR MAJESTY, WHY DO YOU KEEP REFERRING TO *BANJO* AS "*KRAMPUS?*"

BECAUSE THAT'S WHAT HE *IS*.

HMM, I'VE *NEVER* HEARD OF THAT TYPE OF MONKEY BEFORE.

IS *THAT* WHAT HE TOLD YOU HE WAS?
INTERESTING.

HEY GUYS, WHAT'CHA WHISPERIN' ABOUT UP THERE?
THWAK
SILENCE!
WILL WE BE SAFE WHERE WE'RE GOING?
PROBABLY NOT.
GREAT.
DON'T WORRY ABOUT THE SHROMPH, TURTLE. WE'LL BE OKAY.
IT'S NOT THE SHROMPH I'M WORRIED ABOUT.

THEY SHOULD BE JUST UP AHEAD.
GOOD, BECAUSE I'M GETTING REALLY TIRED.
WHAT THE...?
CRACK
CRICK
OH, CRAP! IT'S ICE!
CRACK
HOLD ON TIGHT, BUTTONS!

FASTER!
I'D BE *MORE* THAN HAPPY TO TRADE PLACES WITH YOU!

CRACK
CRACK

THAT WAS *TOO* CLOSE!

THIS IS *IT?*

YOU JUST TOOK THE WORDS RIGHT OUT OF MY MOUTH.

WITH ALL THE TUNNELS LEADING INTO THIS ROOM, IT'S GONNA BE HARD TO DEFEND OURSELVES.
STUPID KRAMPUS.
I'M SORRY, KRAMPUS, IF OUR HOME DOESN'T PLEASE YOU.

EXCUSE ME, YOUR MAJESTY! I AGREE WITH BANJO!
REALLY?

DO YOU HAVE ANY WEAPONS WE COULD USE TO DEFEND OURSELVES WITH?
I LIKE HOW YOU THINK.

WHAT DID YOU HAVE IN MIND?

ANYTHING SHARP AND POINTY!
ARE THERE ANY MORE OF THOSE SPEAR THINGIES?

OH, THOSE. WELL, WE ONLY HAVE TEN OF THEM, SO WE'LL HAVE TO SHARE.

HOW CAN THIS GET ANY WORSE?

MAJESTY! YOUR MAJESTY!
I SAW HIM! HE'S COMING!

YOU HAD TO ASK?

WHICH WAY?
THEY'RE COMING DOWN *THAT* TUNNEL, MAJESTY.

ALL SHROMPH GET BEHIND ME!

HE WON'T TAKE US ALIVE!

THAT IS *ONE* CONFIDENT SHROMPH!

STEADY SHROMPH! HOLD YOUR GROUND!

Thunk
Thunk

TRY NOT TO GET KILLED.
THAT SOUNDS LIKE CONCERN.
NOT AT ALL.

Thunk
THUNK
Thunk

ABE! BANJO! MEG! YOU'RE ALL SAFE!

CHICKENHARE! YOU'RE ALIVE!
AND HE BROUGHT US A DEAD GOAT.

HOLD ON, HE'S WITH US.

THERE'S NO TIME! WE HAVE TO LEAVE RIGHT NOW!

WE THOUGHT THE TAXIDERMIST GOT YOU.

WHAT'S WITH THE GOAT?

UH...THE GOAT'S A LONG STORY.
HELLO, YOUR MAJESTY.
MR. BUTTONS?
YOU LOOK TERRIBLE.

I TAKE IT YOU TWO KNOW EACH OTHER?
WE GO WAY BACK.

*SERIOUSLY,* GUYS, WE NEED TO GET OUT OF HERE! THE TAXIDER...

...MIST.

YES?
WHAT *ABOUT* THE TAXIDERMIST?

HE'S STANDING RIGHT BEHIND YOU!

AND YOU'RE ALL INVITED BACK TO MY PLACE FOR TEA AND STUFFING!

YOU'RE NOT WELCOME HERE, KLAUS!
GET OUT!

NOT WITHOUT WHAT BELONGS TO ME!

THERE'S NOTHING HERE FOR YOU, KLAUS!

THAT'S WHERE YOU'RE *MISTAKEN*, MONKEY!

YOU SEE, I PAID FOR THE CHICKEN-BUNNY AND THE HAIRY TURTLE FAIR AND SQUARE.

*BEARDED*! NOT HAIRY!

AND AS FOR YOU, *MONKEY*...

I CAUGHT YOU AND YOUR GIRLFRIEND ON MY LAST HUNTING EXPEDITION. THAT MAKES YOU *MINE* AS WELL.

AND I'LL BE TAKING THE SHROMPH TOO BECAUSE... WELL, BECAUSE SHROMPH JUST TASTE SO DARN GOOD WITH SALT AND BUTTER.
I HATE BUTTER.

GOT ANY BIG IDEAS?
WORKING ON IT.

GO GET'EM, BOYS!

SHROMPH! ATTACK!

I'LL TAKE THE TWINS!
GOOD, BECAUSE I WANT THE BUTLER!

SMACK

MEG!

I'LL *TAKE* IT FROM HERE, THANKS!
BE MY GUEST.

I WOULD *NOT* WANT TO BE THAT *BUTLER* RIGHT NOW.

WAIT HERE! I'M GONNA HELP MY FRIENDS!

I HAVE FOUR BROKEN LEGS, REMEMBER? WHERE WOULD I GO?

YOU LIKE THAT PIG-BOY?

MERCY! MERCY!

GET OFF ME!

OOF!

YOU ALL RIGHT, *ABE?*

FABULOUS!

LOOKIN' GOOD, *MEG!*
THANKS!
THEY'RE NOT SUPPOSED TO BEND THAT WAY!

I'VE HAD JUST ABOUT ENOUGH OF YOU, YOUR ROYAL HIGHNESS!
UNHAND ME, BRUTE!

MAYBE I'LL JUST UNHEAD YOU, INSTEAD!

NO!

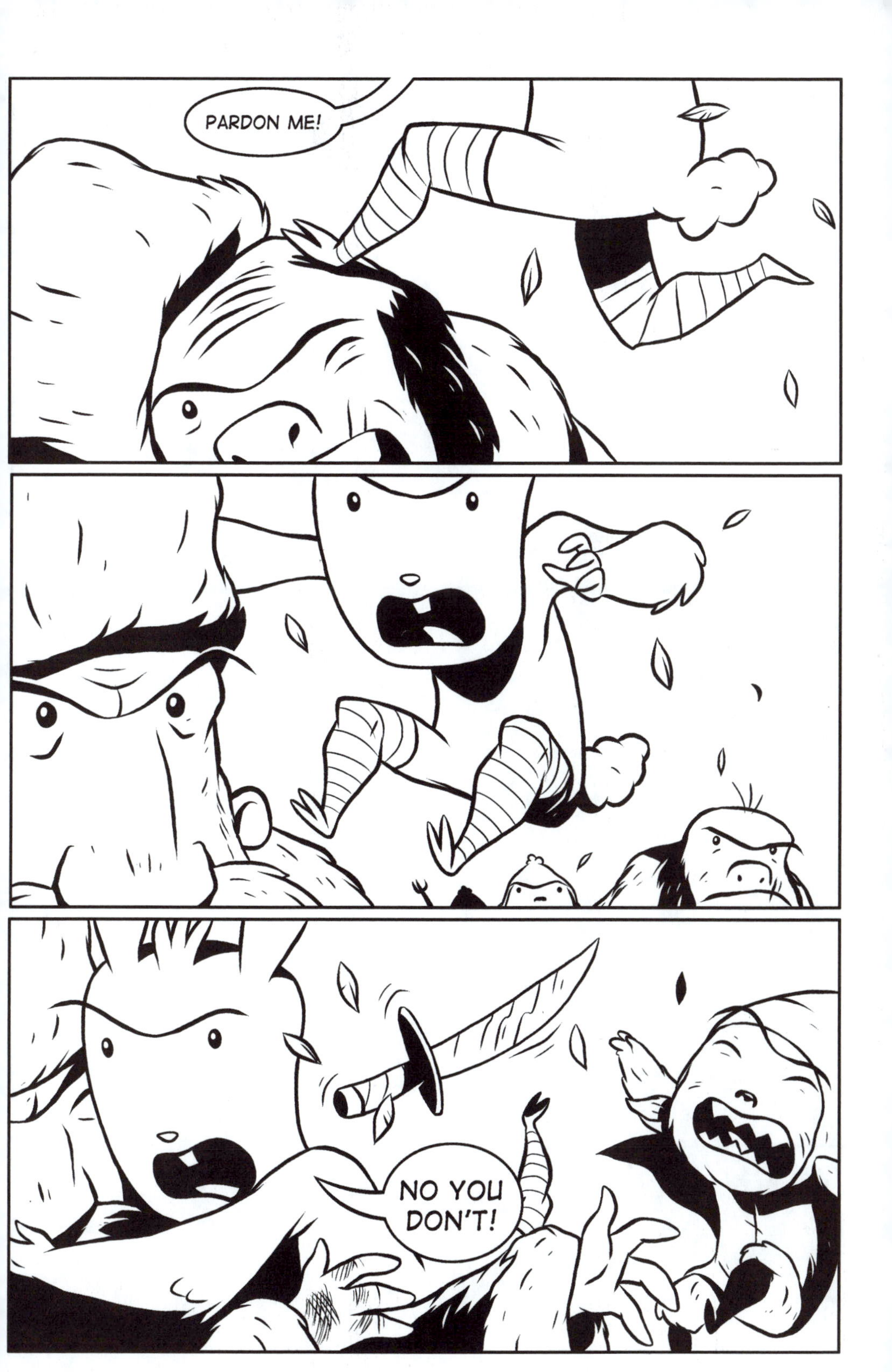
PARDON ME!
NO YOU DON'T!

I WON'T LET YOU HURT ANYONE ELSE, *KLAUS*!

IT'S *OVER!*

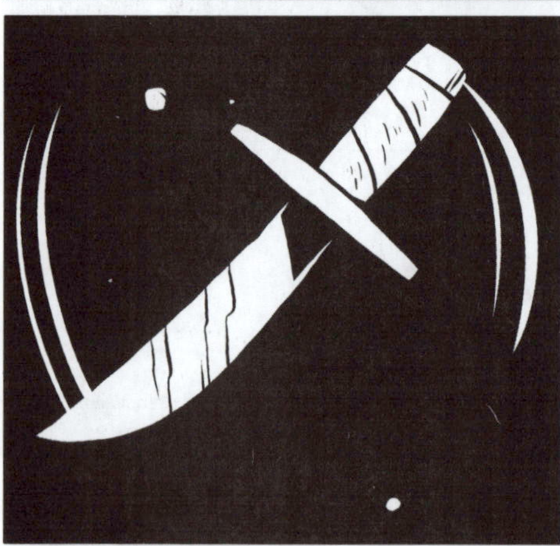

KA-CHUNK!

AAUGH!
FASTER, PIGGY!

STUPID, BRAVE CHICKEN-BUNNY!
CRUNCH

NO! STOP!

DID YOU *HONESTLY* THINK YOU AND YOUR FRIENDS COULD REALLY STOP ME?
DOESN'T THAT HURT?
NOT AT ALL!

MASTER... MASTER... STOP... PLEASE.
WHAT?
DO YOU WANNA BE NEXT...?
IT CAN'T BE!
WHY DID YOU STAB ME, MASTER? I THOUGHT YOU LOVED ME.
MR. BUTTONS! YOU'RE...YOU'RE ALIVE!

WHAT HAVE I *DONE?*
I DIDN'T KNOW...
I'LL...I'LL GET YOU HELP!

PLEASE HURRY...
...SO... COLD.

*CHICKENHARE,* ARE YOU OKAY?
I'LL BE FINE.
WHAT *NOW?*
*FINGERBONES!* HELP, I NEED YOU!

I HAVE AN IDEA.

WAKE UP!
SLAP
BETTER LATE THAN NEVER!

WAKE UP, YOU IDIOT! I NEED YOUR HELP!
...BUT I DON'T WANT TO WEAR THE RED DRESS, MOM.

SHROMPH!
I DEMAND THAT YOU HELP ME!

SOMEBODY... PLEASE.

DADDY WON'T LET YOU DIE, *MR. BUTTONS!*

BUTTONS?
WHERE'D YOU GO?

HEY, *KLAUS*! THOSE GUYS TOOK YOUR GOAT. THEY SAID THEY WERE GONNA *KILL* IT!

WHAT!

THEY WENT DOWN *THAT TUNNEL*.

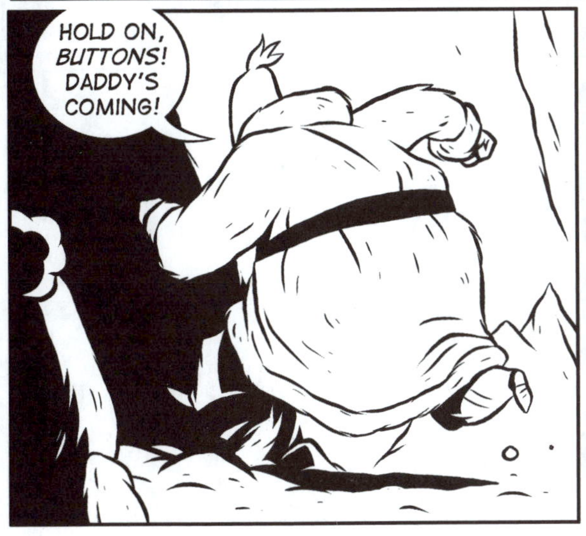
HOLD ON, *BUTTONS*! DADDY'S COMING!

I *SURE* HOPE THEY KNOW WHAT THEY'RE DOING.

FASTER! HE'S *RIGHT* BEHIND US!
WHY DID I GET *THIS* END?
IT'S JUST UP AHEAD!
ALRIGHT, BANJO, LETS SET 'ER DOWN... GENTLY.

LET HIM GO!

NEVER!

MASTER! SAVE ME, PLEASE! THEY'RE GONNA DO AWFUL THINGS TO ME!
SHE'S OURS NOW, *KLAUS*!

SAVE ME, MASTER! PLEASE!

YOU THREE BETTER GET OUTTA HERE. HE LOOKS *REALLY PISSED*!

ARE YOU SURE?

I'M SURE. GO.

MASTER, HELP! I'M SO SCARED!
TINK

YOU COWARDS WON'T GET FAR!

DADDY'S GOT YOU NOW, *BUTTONS*. EVERYTHING'S OKAY.
TINK

TINK
CRACK
WHAT?!
CRACK
TINK
CRICK

aaauuuGGHH!
CRACK
CRACK
CRACK

GUYS!

ABE, STOP!
IT'S ICE! STAY THERE, WE'LL BE RIGHT OVER.

WHAT HAPPENED?
WHERE'S KLAUS?

IT'S OVER.
THE GOAT SAVED US.

HEY, YEAH! WHERE IS THAT GUY? I THINK HE ATE MY *HAT*.

SHE'S *GONE*.

SHE FELL THROUGH THE ICE, ALONG WITH *KLAUS*.

I'M SURE SHE DIDN'T FEEL ANYTHING, CHICKENHARE.
YEAH. SHE WAS ALREADY DEAD, REMEMBER?

THE ONLY THING I'M FEELING IS OVERWHELMING GRATITUDE.
I CAN'T THANK YOU GUYS ENOUGH FOR WHAT YOU'VE DONE.

THEY'RE RIGHT, CHICKENHARE.

I'M JUST HAPPY IT'S OVER.
THERE'S JUST *ONE* LAST THING I NEED YOU TO DO FOR ME, OKAY?
LET ABE HAVE MY HAT. I THINK I ATE HIS DURING THE FIGHT.
*WAIT!* HOW COME *ABE* GETS ALL THE HATS?
I'LL MAKE SURE HE GETS IT.
STUPID *ABE*! STUPID GOAT!
MY SPIRIT CAN FINALLY REST. THANK YOU.
YOU'RE WELCOME.

THANKS AGAIN FOR ALL THE HOSPITALITY, YOUR HIGHNESS. ESPECIALLY THE WARM CLOAKS.
DON'T FORGET THE HUGE BAG OF LEFTOVERS!
IT CERTAINLY WAS QUITE A DELICIOUS FEAST, WASN'T IT?

THE SHROMPH ARE FOREVER INDEBTED TO YOU FOR SAVING US FROM *KLAUS*.

AND WE TO YOU, MAJESTY.

I WISH WE COULD STAY LONGER, BUT ABE AND I HAVE SOME BUSINESS TO ATTEND TO BACK HOME.
WE UNDERSTAND.

MMM

I DO HAVE ONE QUESTION THOUGH.
WHAT HAPPENED TO THE OTHER ONES?

I'M NOT SURE I'M FOLLOWING YOU.

THE BUTLER? AND THE GUYS THAT LOOKED LIKE PIGS?
WHAT HAPPENED TO THEM?
OH, THEM!

I BELIEVE YOUR FRIEND IS FINISHING THE LAST OF THEM RIGHT NOW.

LIKE I SAID, IT WAS *QUITE* A *FEAST*!

OH, WELL.

WELL, I GUESS WE SHOULD BE ON OUR WAY. HUH, *ABE?*
ABSOLUTELY!
UH...HEY, *CHICKENHARE*...
...ANY CHANCE I MIGHT BE ABLE TO TAG ALONG FOR A WHILE?
SURE. IF YOU WANT TO.

AND ME TOO?
WHY DO YOU WANT TO COME WITH US?
LET'S CALL IT UNFINISHED BUSINESS.
HEY... I THOUGHT WE WERE PAST ALL THAT?
SUCKS TO BE YOU, PAL!
THANKS AGAIN, MAJESTY.

I WANT YOU TO TAKE OUR BOAT TO HELP YOU ON YOUR WAY.
SCABBY HERE IS AN AMAZING CAPTAIN. HE'LL SEE YOU HOME SAFELY.

THANKS, MAJESTY.

SHALL WE BE OFF THEN?
THE BOAT BE HALF A DAY'S JOURNEY AWAY.

HOW MUCH FURTHER 'TIL WE GET TO THE BOAT?
IT'S NOT FAR NOW, KRAMPUS.

I STILL CAN'T BELIEVE *BUTTONS* WANTED ME TO HAVE HER HAT.
ONLY BECAUSE SHE KNEW YOU WOULD BE LAME ENOUGH TO ACTUALLY WEAR IT.

*BANJO*, HOLD UP A SECOND.
WHAT FOR?
LOOK. THERE'S THE SHORE.

WHAT IS IT, *MEG*?
YOU NEED TO TELL THEM, *BANJO*. OR ELSE I WILL!

WHAT DO YOU MEAN?
THEY DESERVE TO KNOW EXACTLY WHO, AND WHAT YOU ARE.

LOOK, YOU'RE PUTING THEM IN DANGER BY TAGGING ALONG.
ME? WHAT ABOUT YOU?

YOU'RE RIGHT... I NEVER REALLY CONSIDERED THAT.

COME ON, YOU TWO!

THE BOAT'S JUST UP AHEAD, GUYS.

HEY, *WHO'S* HUNGRY?

*HOW* CAN YOU *POSSIBLY* BE HUNGRY AFTER ALL THAT *"BUTLER"* YOU ATE EARLIER?

HOW CAN *YOU* WEAR A HAT THAT WAS WORN BY A DEAD *GOAT*?

TOUCHÉ!
WHY THANK YOU.

HOPEFULLY OUR JOURNEY HOME WILL BE FAR MORE RELAXING...
I'M SURE IT WILL BE!
THE END

SPECIAL THANKS TO
ROBYN FABSITS,
MIKE GAFFNEY,
KERRY CALLEN,
&
SHAWNA GORE

WITHOUT THEIR SUPPORT CHICKENHARE WOULD
STILL BE LIVING ONLY IN THE PAGES OF
MY SKETCHBOOK.

THANKS ALSO TO
JOHN DAWBARN,
SYLVIA CHRISTIANSON,
TONY NOWAKOWSKI,
CHRIS HARDING,
JACK PULLAN,
PETE WHITEHEAD,
&
JASON GRINE

# Looking for something new to read?

**CHECK OUT THESE OTHER GREAT TITLES FROM DARK HORSE BOOKS!**

Join Usagi Yojimbo in his hare-raising adventures of life and death. Watch as he faces assassins, medicine peddlers, bat ninjas, and more, in this twenty-volumes-and-counting epic! This is a story of honor and adventure, a masterful adaptation of samurai legend to sequential art. Dark Horse is proud to present this Eisner award-winning and internationally acclaimed tour de force by master storyteller Stan Sakai!

## Little Lulu®

Lulu Moppet is the true-blue daughter of Main Street America, clever and sweet, mischievous and generous, an eight-year-old hero for anyone who ever wanted to bring home a gorilla, scare the pants off of ghosts, and outwit every grownup in sight. With eleven volumes already available (and many more, including a color special, on the way!), there are plenty of chances to discover why generations of readers have considered *Little Lulu* one of smartest, cutest, and funniest comics ever to hit the shelves!

## Sock Monkey™

Just how much trouble can a toy animal really cause? Find out in this funny, unsettling, and utterly endearing series written and drawn by Tony Millionaire! Follow along with mischievous sock monkey Uncle Gabby and bumbling bird Drinky Crow as they try to find a home for a shrunken head, try their hands at matchmaking, hunt salamanders and butterflies, tackle home repairs, face off against creatures from the deep, and try to get to heaven. Delights! Happy endings and random destruction are guaranteed! Check out any of the amazing *Sock Monkey* stories already out and about, or hop on board for the latest *Sock Monkey* yarn, *The Inches Incident*.

**Find out more about these and other great Dark Horse all-ages titles at darkhorse.com!**

AVAILABLE AT YOUR LOCAL COMICS SHOP OR BOOKSTORE
TO FIND A COMICS SHOP IN YOUR AREA, CALL 1-888-266-4226

For more information or to order direct: •On the web: darkhorse.com •E-mail: mailorder@darkhorse.com •Phone: 1-800-862-0052 Mon.-Fri. 9 A.M. to 5 P.M. Pacific Time.